Good News - Bad News

Leadership Challenges for Servant Leaders

John J. Sullivan

Other books by John J. Sullivan

Servant First! Leadership for the New Millennium, Xulon Press, 2004

Seven Virtues, The Adventures of John Mouse, Xulon Press, 2010

Books in the series, Leadership Challenges for Servant Leaders:

My Betrayer is at Hand, CreateSpace, 2012

Details, Details, Details, CreateSpace, 2012

Truth Telling, CreateSpace, 2012

Severing the Ties That Bind, CreateSpace, 2012

Good News -- Bad News, CreateSpace, 2012

Dedicated to leaders
who are not afraid
to speak the truth --
with grace

Preface

This is the fifth monograph in a series which addresses the most common leadership challenges in organizations today. Although the challenges are similar across organizations, the leadership styles which confront them are varied.

Leadership is leadership, whether one leads a small fellowship group or a large corporation, a squad or a corps, a team or an institution. What changes are the language (terms, acronyms) and the rules of engagement (how you interact with followers).

Interestingly, the more senior one becomes the more important are interpersonal relationships. This is counterintuitive at first glance but consider that as one leads larger and more complex organizations one becomes less and less an expert in what the organization does. The further one gets from "the product" the less one knows the product. Senior leaders become increasingly dependent upon followers who have the product expertise they lack; therefore the ability to build and maintain strong interpersonal relationships with core individuals within organizations is key to upper mobility and senior leader success.

This series is aimed at servant leaders or what Jim Collins calls Level 5 leaders[1]. This leadership model is best exemplified by the leadership style of Jesus of Nazareth who said He came to serve and not to be served. Leaders in industry, government, not-for-profit organizations and churches are discovering that

---

[1] Collins, Jim, *Good to Great: Why Some Companies Make the Leap . . . and Others Don't*, HarperCollins, 2001

the servant leader model is highly effective across organizational types.

This upside-down leadership style puts the needs of followers above those of the leader; promotes teamwork, individual dignity and worth; and results in a synergy of purpose unachievable with the old leadership models. Its application in today's organizations creates an environment in which people freely choose to create, innovate, and strive for excellence.

Enjoy this monograph on performance evaluation and look for more books in this series *Leadership Challenges for Servant Leaders*.

Contents

Introduction

Why do performance evaluation? What purpose does it serve? How often should leaders evaluate the performance of subordinates? How should they obtain performance information to make the evaluation? What method should they use to discriminate between different people's performance? How does the leader tell people bad news without destroying their egos? Aren't most performance evaluations meaningless in terms of true "evaluation?" Let's take these questions one at a time.

Why do performance evaluation? Performance evaluation can be a powerful tool for leaders to help people become more productive, efficient, and effective. In short, their main purpose must be to help people grow. But they must be done right or they will do more harm then good. Jack Stack, president and CEO of Springfield Remanufacturing Corporation, agrees that, "...the typical annual–review process...creates divisions, undermines morale, makes people angry, jealous, and cynical. It unleashes a whole lot of negative energy and the organization gets nothing in return" (Stack, 1997). Many people facing the annual performance evaluation are filled with fear and trembling especially when the evaluation is the first and only time they have received performance feedback during the year. Add that lack of feedback to a coupling of the performance evaluation with future pay and promotion, and people are often terrorized by the thought of the interview. Most leaders do not go to the extremes that Admiral Hyman Rickover, the father of the U.S. nuclear Navy, was famous for (more on that later) but suffice to say that the experience is often an unpleasant one for most people, and this includes leaders.

Fear of the interview sometimes leads to aberrant behavior on the part of the person being interviewed manifested by lying, exaggeration, blame displacement, or simply tuning out. Under these conditions, no learning takes place and future growth is stymied.

1

What is the Purpose?

Performance evaluation should be for the purpose of helping people perform at a higher level. For the servant leader it should be a primary function of helping people to reach their full potential and true job satisfaction. It should involve measurement of goal achievement against previously agreed upon objectives and metrics. Where goals were not attained, we ask why not? Where they were achieved, we ask why? Was it due to what we did, did not do, or just luck? The answer to these questions will determine what changes, if any, we need to make to processes. Where goals were not achieved, leaders should ask the person being evaluated to explain the cause. Deming reminds us that 85% of the time (he later changed it to 96%) problems are due to the process and not the person (Deming, 1986). Leaders are responsible for the processes. Therefore, leaders

> Performance evaluation should be for the purpose of helping people perform at a higher level

must determine what tools or process changes are required to improve performance. For example, several years ago a salesman told me of his frustration to achieve ever increasing goals imposed by his supervisor while he continued to deny him use of a cell phone. He explained that he could use his time much more efficiently with a cell phone to insure that his contacts were available when he called on them.

Determining *what* to evaluate is the first step in creating an effective performance evaluation. Are we going to evaluate *traits* (viz. stable aspects of people, closely related to personality), *behavior* (viz. what people actually do on the job), or *results* (viz. what people accomplish) (DuBrin, 2003). In most cases the best performance appraisal systems will rely mainly on evaluating results as these can be done objectively. The essential job functions to be measured must come from the tasks, duties, and responsibilities defined in the person's job description. Performance standards should be included in the job description which clearly states what performance is considered satisfactory in each area of the job (Mathis and Jackson, 1999). Evaluating a person on duties that are not part of the job description is not valid. Therefore, it is incumbent upon leaders to periodically review their employee's job descriptions to ensure that as duties change over time, these are reflected in their job descriptions.

2

When to Evaluate?

True "performance evaluation" should happen every day, assuming leaders have daily contact with their people. If contact is less frequent, performance evaluation should occur whenever contact is made with the person. This informal feedback can be as simple as a compliment or correction on job performance yet is a powerful tool to encourage increased productivity. Daily, weekly, monthly, and quarterly goals may obviate the need for an annual review. The first time a person learns that his performance is not meeting goals should not be at the annual review. With short interval goals, each person knows exactly where they stand throughout the year.

It is virtually impossible for leaders—with the possible exception of very small businesses—to truly observe any employee's overall performance over a period of

> It is virtually impossible for leaders to truly observe any employee's overall performance over a period of time

time.   Therefore, relying only on your own observations will tell just part of the story. A too common method is the "manager's notebook" where critical incidents are recorded (usually only the "bad" occurrences) and then used to form the evaluation. This method does not take into account a person's overall performance day-to-day and focuses on exceptions to behavior. It is as faulty as using varying standards to evaluate different people, applying greater weight to recent occurrences, or the "halo effect." This rater error is present when the leader rates the employee high or low on all items because of one characteristic (e.g., friendly, funny, or personable) (Mathis and Jackson, 1999).

3

How Can We Know?

How, then, is the leader to obtain a true picture of performance? Objective goal measurement is one way. Another is to obtain input, albeit often subjective, from several different sources. This is commonly called a "360 degree appraisal." It means that you get input from peers, suppliers, customers and even the employee herself before forming the evaluation. Granted, this is time-consuming and perhaps expensive, but it allows the leader to see what others perceive as the true performance of an employee. When reviewing the input from multiple sources, leaders should try to form an overall picture of the person's performance rather than focus on specifics within an externally obtained evaluation realizing that some distortion of performance is common.

A senior leader of a large multi-national corporation once told me that before he visits his senior managers around the world, he first visits their major customers and asks for an evaluation of the performance of the local office. He said this helps him to "cut through the hype" when determining the effectiveness of his outlying staff.

Good News - Bad News

Some organizations require leaders to directly compare the performance of their employees against one another (Mathis and Jackson, 1999). These ranking and forced distribution methods are artificial and often arbitrary. Ranking people from highest to lowest or within a certain category to achieve the classic bell curve is not helpful and often perceived as being cruel. If Deming is correct that most people's performance is within three standard deviations of average, than only a very small percentage are either truly exceptional or truly poor (Deming, 1986).

4

Bearing Bad News

How can the leader be the bearer of bad news without destroying either the output or ego of his/her employee, and how can he make performance evaluation meaningful to both parties?

No one likes to be the bearer of bad news--including leaders. That is why performance evaluation is among the greatest leadership failings. How does the servant

> No one likes to be the bearer of bad news

leader deliver bad news while demonstrating his concern for the welfare of the person being evaluated? Leaders are *not* being kind or sympathetic by *not* pointing out performance problems as these may lead to the eventual loss of the job. But it must be done in a way that the person hears and understands the problem and helps to create a plan for correction. William Rosenzweig, Managing Director of Venture Strategy Group, says truth telling is rare "because so many of us take the most well-intentioned criticism personally. The only way to unleash open communication is to convince people that honesty is about group learning, not individual criticism (Muoio, 2007). It all begins with setting the stage.

As we've said, performance evaluation should be a tool to help people grow. It is one tool, not the only tool, and it is a powerful one--if done correctly. First, we make the assumption that the leader and the employee have met prior to the start of the evaluation period and agreed upon a set of SMART goals (i.e., specific, measureable, achievable, results-oriented, and time-determined). Second, these are then measured over the evaluation period (e.g., 6 months) with a set of agreed upon metrics that are charted or otherwise displayed. Whether or not the goals are achieved can readily be ascertained with reference to the data. This method eliminates any subjective evaluation and surprises.

Major findings of years of research on performance evaluation indicate that people are most satisfied with the system when they participate in the process (DuBrin, 2003). Accordingly, Peter Drucker suggests subordinates write a "manager's letter" twice a year (Drucker, 2001). This letter is one way for subordinates to participate in the development of objectives and goals for their area of responsibility. To help people to assume a "sense of participation" or ownership, the manager's letter sets out the performance standards that the subordinate believes apply to him. Then he lists the things he must do to achieve those goals and what obstacles he must overcome within his own unit.

Jack Stack, as president and CEO, establishes standards, goals and accountabilities for about 25 people in his company. However, this is not done in isolation. "We decide *together* what expectations we'll have about their performance in the coming year, and we try to quantify as many of those as possible" (Stack, 1997, *emphasis* added).

If a goal was achieved, we ask why? Was it due to something we did, e.g., a process refinement, more experience (less time to complete a task as tasks are repeated), or just luck? If we did not achieve a goal, again we ask why? Do we need to improve the process? Was the goal unrealistically high? Did circumstances beyond our control alter the environment (e.g., Hurricane Katrina)? Or were we just unlucky? The answers to these questions may not be readily apparent and the employee should come to the evaluation with data to explain why goals were or were not achieved.

Stack takes a rather uncommon approach to goal achievement in that although he keeps a close watch on progress during the year, he restrains himself from taking any action for nine months. He says that, "I've watched too many managers stumble at first and then go on to have a great year, and it often takes three full quarters before you begin to see the results" (Stack, 1997).

When goals are not achieved, leaders have the opportunity to teach, coach, and help employees to improve their performance. Remember to critique the work not the individual. A servant leader always has the other person's needs in mind and truly wants them to succeed. In other words, you must be clear that you are not saying "you are a bad/lazy/unskilled person," rather "that your output can be improved by doing the following ..." Nearly everyone wants to improve, develop expertise, and have a sense of satisfaction in their work. It is up to you, the leader, to create an environment where people can achieve job satisfaction and feel they are an important part of the "team."

Telling people the "bad news" is an important responsibility for leaders. You are not doing your people favors by not telling them when they are making mistakes or not working up to expectations. *How* you tell them will determine what they do about what you say. Do not be confused with a leader's responsibility to maintain discipline and the requirement to evaluate performance. Discipline problems must be addressed separately and immediately and according to a published set of rules governing conduct. For instance, a person who is frequently late to work is a discipline problem and must be handled according to organizational policy and work rules. Job performance is what we are discussing here and it is distinct from discipline.

If the leader has been measuring goal performance during the evaluation period, she should not wait until the formal evaluation to coach, teach, demonstrate, or suggest ways to improve output especially when it appears that output is not on track to achieve a goal. She should be aware, at least on a monthly basis, whether output is on, behind, or ahead of schedule and provide input to improve performance, as needed.

If the performance evaluation is to be effective it must be non-threatening

The formal performance evaluation provides a time when the two parties can sit down and discuss, analyze and evaluate goal performance. Where goals were not achieved even after frequent input from the leader, a detailed process evaluation may be called for.

John J. Sullivan

If the performance evaluation is to be truly effective, it must be non-threatening. That means that discussion of pay or promotion should be done separately from this meeting. When people know that a raise or promotion is on the line, they will not be as forthcoming about their own inadequacies, lack of training or understanding. If you want the evaluation to be more than just a one-way conversation, you must divorce pay/promotion from performance (Deming, 1986).

Good News - Bad News

5

Set the Stage

Finally, the setting for the discussion is important. Again, it should be non-threatening. Few leaders go to the extremes that Admiral Rickover was famous for, (allegedly he sat behind a desk on a raised dais and the poor petitioner was seated in an uncomfortable chair where the two front legs had been shortened, facing him), but even subtle hints can create anxiety in the evaluatee. Both parties should be on equal ground, e.g., adjacent easy chairs, and the leader needs to begin to put the employee at ease by warmly welcoming them by name. Watch your body language so as to not send threatening signals (e.g., arms tightly crossed). Initially asking questions about family, a recent vacation or the like can help to reduce anxiety. When it appears that the person is relaxing, the evaluator should begin by asking him how *he* thinks his performance has been? Often, you will be surprised at how brutally honest people will be and much tougher on themselves than you are. After listening to their response and perhaps asking a few questions, the leader should sum up the person's performance in a few sentences. (Some like to do the summation at the end of the evaluation but doing it first tends to remove fear, especially when they hear good news!)

Begin by telling the person something positive about their performance. Just as no one likes to hear bad things *everyone* likes to hear good things about themselves. By beginning with positive comments people will be listening to what you say. We all get defensive when confronted with criticism of our performance and some will simply stop listening if the leader begins with negative feedback. After telling them the "good" then move on to the "other."

> Just as no one likes to hear bad things, everyone likes to hear good things about themselves

When critiquing performance that is not meeting standards or goals, remember to be objective and avoid appearing to attack the individual. Demonstrate by your words and body language that you respect the person being evaluated and want the best for them. Offer suggestions and to work with the person to develop a plan for achieving their goals. Set a time to get back together again, normally within the next sixty days, to review the plan. Try to end the meeting on a high note assuring the person that you support them and want them to excel.

With proper planning, courage to tell the truth and a genuine concern for the welfare of their people, servant leaders can transform performance evaluations from something dreaded by both parties into a learning experience. Don't be surprised if you, the leader, are the real learner!

John J. Sullivan

References

Deming, W., (1986), *Out of the Crisis*, Cambridge, MA: MIT

Drucker, P., (2001), *The Essential Drucker*, New York: Harper Collins

DuBrin, A., (2003), *Essentials of Management, Sixth Edition*, Mason, OH: South-Western

Mathis, R. and Jackson, J., (1999), *Human Resource Management*, Cincinnati, OH: South-Western College Publishing

Muoio, A., (2007), *The Truth Is, the Truth Hurts*, FastCompany.com, http://www.fastcompany.com/magazine/14/one.html, accessed May 15, 2008

Stack, J. (1997), "The Curse of the Annual Performance Review," *Inc. Magazine*, March 1997

Good News - Bad News

John J. Sullivan

About the Author

John J. Sullivan is the director of ServantLeader Ministries whose mission is to educate, encourage and equip leaders in all walks of life who desire to serve rather than be served.

He has had a wide variety of career experiences. He has served as a Marine Corps fighter pilot, a squadron and air station commander, senior staff officer, consultant, quality examiner, athletics director, professor, and conference commissioner. He is widely acclaimed as an authority on servant leadership as an author, a teacher and a practitioner.

A highly decorated Vietnam veteran, prior to entering academia he served for 28 years in the U.S. Marine Corps as a helicopter gunship pilot, fighter pilot, squadron commander, senior staff officer, base commander, and professor, retiring as a colonel. As a senior staff officer in the Pentagon, he was Program Coordinator for what was then the Department of the Navy's largest development and acquisition program, the F/A-18 Hornet aircraft. While he was the Commanding Officer, Marine Corps Air Station Beaufort, SC, the base was selected in worldwide competition as the best installation in the Marine Corps and received the prestigious Commander-in-Chief's Award for Installation Excellence.

He was the Course Director of Policy Making and Implementation within the National Security Decision Making Department and professor of management at the Naval War College, Newport, RI. He taught in the graduate program primarily in leadership education.

Good News - Bad News

An American Society for Quality Certified Quality Manager, he was a founder of the Rhode Island Area Coalition for Excellence (RACE), helped design its State quality award, and was its first lead examiner.

Following his military career, Sullivan served for nine years as an associate professor of business at Montreat College, Montreat, NC. His teaching focus was in the disciplines of leadership and management.

He is a graduate of the University of Southern California, Webster University and the Naval War College.

Visit http://www.servantleaderministries.org for more information on servant leadership or the author.